NOT FROM HERE, NOT FROM THERE

The Forced Migration of American Citizens

Maria Teresa H. de Holcomb

ISBN: 1508755728
ISBN 13: 9781508755722
Library of Congress Control Number: 2015903741
CreateSpace Independent Publishing Platform
North Charleston, South Carolina

Dedicated to all Americans and Mexicans who suffered through the repatriation period and to my son, Edward, who informed me about this often-forgotten period of history.

CHARACTERS

GRANDPA JUAN, an elderly man
GRANDMA LUPE, an elderly woman
ROBERTITO, grandson of Juan and Lupe, a young boy
LUPE, Juan's wife, a woman in her late twenties, and then older
JUAN, a man in his early thirties, and then older
YOUNG ROBERT, son of Juan and Lupe, a young boy
YOUNG PATTY, daughter of Juan and Lupe, a young girl
PABLO, a man in his late twenties, and then older
MAN'S VOICE
ANOTHER MAN'S VOICE
GRANDMA, an elderly woman (nonspeaking role)
MEXICAN BORDER PATROL AGENT, a man in his forties
Two MEN (nonspeaking roles)
MAN AT THE BORDER
SARA, Pablo's wife, a woman in her late twenties, and then older
YOUNG FERNANDO, son of Pablo and Sara, a young boy
(nonspeaking role)
CANDELARIA, a woman in her thirties, and then older
CARLOS, Candelaria's husband, in his thirties, and then older
(nonspeaking role)
CONDUCTOR, a man in his sixties, and CONDUCTOR'S
VOICE
WOMAN'S VOICE

FRANK, a teenager
ANTHONY, a teenager
ANTHONY'S MOTHER, a woman in her thirties
FRANK'S MOTHER, a woman in her thirties
OFFICER, a man in his fifties
PREGNANT WOMAN, in her late twenties
PATTY, Juan and Lupe's daughter as a teenager
ROBERT, Juan and Lupe's son as a teenager
FERNANDO, Pablo and Sara's son as a teenager
MRS. SMITH, a woman in her midforties
MEGAN, a woman in her twenties
NUN, an elderly woman
TODDLER BOY (nonspeaking role)

LOCATION

United States
Mexico

TIME

1930 to 1942 and present day

ACT I

<u>Scene 1</u>

Lights rise on a living room. Robertito enters and kisses Grandpa Juan and Grandma Lupe on the cheek.

GRANDPA JUAN
Sit down, Robertito. Tell us about school. What did you learn today?

ROBERTITO
Something so sad. In 1942, they put the Japanese people in inter...something.

GRANDPA JUAN
Internment camps.

ROBERTITO
Yes, internment. I feel so sorry for those people.

GRANDMA LUPE
(sadly)
The Japanese experienced internment. We experienced repatriation.

ROBERTITO
What is that?

1

GRANDPA JUAN
It was 1930. We were sent to Mexico.

ROBERTITO
I wonder why my history book doesn't say anything about it.

GRANDPA JUAN
Sometimes it is better not to mention the past.

GRANDMA LUPE
Robertito, these memories are very painful for us.

ROBERTITO
I don't understand. Your parents, grandparents, and great-grandparents were born in this country. They are American citizens. You were not repatriated, correct?

GRANDMA LUPE
Yes, we were. We were among more than a million and a half. And we were American citizens.

ROBERTITO
Tell me more, Grandma.

GRANDMA LUPE
(*drying her tears*)
Another day, Robertito, another day.

Blackout.

Scene 2

Lights rise. Lupe is tending to Young Robert and Young Patty in a nicely decorated living room. Juan enters.

> JUAN
> Lupe, come to the bedroom. I have to tell you something.

Lupe follows him to the corner of the stage. The children play in the background.

> LUPE
> What is wrong? You seem so agitated.

> JUAN
> You are not going to believe what is going on here.

> LUPE
> I have not listened to the radio today. Tell me.

> JUAN
> Repatriation!

> LUPE
> Slow down. I don't know what you are saying.

> JUAN
> *(in a low voice)*
> They are sending us back.

LUPE
To where?

JUAN
To Mexico.

LUPE
I don't understand. We are not illegal. We were born in this country.

JUAN
I know. I know. People of Mexican descent are being forced to leave here. Our great-great-grandparents were born in Mexico, and we still have a Spanish last name.

LUPE
I don't understand. Has President Hoover agreed? My family has been here since the Mexican–American War in 1846.

JUAN
Yes, under the Treaty of Guadalupe Hidalgo.

LUPE
(interrupts)
Stop it! I know all of that. I also know that Mexico lost more than 51 percent of its land to the United States.

JUAN
Yes, and the US government considered us American citizens.

LUPE

So what is the problem? They are sending us to Mexico? We have never been there.

JUAN

I know, but we look Mexican, and our last names are Spanish. Also, they say Mexico is closer to the United States, so it is cheaper to send them back there.

LUPE

Are they sending the Italians? The Hungarians?

JUAN

No.

LUPE

I don't understand. Please tell me what the problem is, the real problem.

JUAN

The high rate of unemployment. The economic situation is so bad for the whole country that people are saying, "If we get rid of the Mexicans, we can have their jobs, and the problem will be solved."

LUPE
(crying)
Mexico was never our country. We don't speak Spanish. We don't have relatives there. This is an injustice. Juan, we are American citizens.

JUAN
(hugging Lupe)
I hate to tell you—the immigration raids
have already started. We have to be ready.
This morning, the neighbors decided to
leave voluntarily.

LUPE
Oh! What about our legal rights?

JUAN
You mean due process? Lupe, there is no
protection for us. We are being pressured to
leave.

LUPE
Forced to leave, you mean. Forced! We are
the scapegoats of the economy.

JUAN
Lupe, do you know why Mexicans are
recruited to work in the United States?

LUPE
They are cheap labor. They are
hardworking, and they don't complain.

JUAN
Agreed. I also heard that employers
are going to be prohibited from hiring
Mexicans. Since they are not going to have
jobs, they have to go so they won't be a
burden on the taxpayers of this country.

LUPE

But Juan, you have a wonderful job. We own our home. We have savings. We help the community.

JUAN

Yes, Lupe, but we fall into one category: undesirable aliens, according to them.

LUPE

Such an injustice.

JUAN

Tomorrow I will withdraw money from the bank.

LUPE

Go now. I have a bad feeling.

Blackout.

Scene 3

Lights rise. Juan is leaving the bank. Pablo rushes over to him.

PABLO

Juan! Juan!

JUAN
(patting him on his back)
Good to see you, Pablo! Are you OK?

PABLO
For now, yes, but I must warn you. The
authorities are coming over to our
neighborhood and knocking on doors. The
Alvarez family did not have time to sell or
take their possessions with them. They are
already gone.

Juan looks around carefully before opening a bag in his hands.

JUAN
Look, Pablo, I took out half of my money.
The bank will send the other half to me
later.

PABLO
When are you leaving?

JUAN
As soon as possible. Things are getting bad.
Listen to the chanting: "Go home, wetbacks.
Let your country feed you. Not ours!" And
the signs: "All Mexicans, go home. We need
your jobs." I must go home and get ready.
How are you getting to Mexico?

PABLO
We are taking the train.

JUAN
I wish you could come with us, but there will
already be five people in my Ford.

> PABLO
> We will see you there.

> JUAN
> I am going to Guanajuato. The land there is very good. I can buy a farm. Bye, Pablo.

Blackout.

Scene 4

Lights rise. Juan and Lupe's living room is full of packed suitcases.

> JUAN
> Lupe, things are getting worse.

> LUPE
> Before you start loading the car, I have to tell you that I am taking my Singer sewing machine. You gave it to me. I love it.

> JUAN
> OK, get it ready. I know how much you love it.

Blackout.

Scene 5

Lights rise on Juan and Lupe's living room. There is a knock at the door. Juan opens it. Pablo enters.

JUAN
Pablo, I just saw you at the bank. Is
everything OK?

PABLO
Do you remember Salvador and Josefina?

JUAN
Of course.

PABLO
They were at the movies. The law
enforcement people came and made all the
Mexicans follow them to the lobby. Salvador
told Josefina to go quickly to the women's
restroom. Salvador went to the men's
restroom. They stayed there for a while.
Later, they found out that the Mexicans who
went to the lobby were taken immediately to
the railroad station. Salvador and Josefina
are fine. I just want to tell you I am leaving
tonight with Sara and my boy, Fernando.
Please be careful.

JUAN
Thanks, Pablo.

They shake hands. Pablo exits.

LUPE
Juan, who was at the door?

JUAN

It was Pablo. Salvador and Josefina were almost detained at the movie theater.

LUPE

(yelling)

I cannot believe this is happening. It is like a nightmare!

JUAN

Tone down, Lupe. I am going out. I will be back soon.

Blackout.

Scene 6

Lights rise dimly on Lupe and Juan's living room. Lupe is pacing back and forth.

LUPE

They have everything wrong. They call it repatriation. It is wrong! Repatriation is returning people to their place of origin. Our origin is here, in the United States. Our country is the United States. Maybe Juan was talking about illegals and got confused with American citizens. Yes, yes. Juan got confused. That is what happened.

Lupe turns on the radio.

MAN'S VOICE

I repeat: Mexicans are taking our jobs. We Americans have rights. We must get our jobs back from these illegals. These Mexicans are breaking the law. They are criminals. When we get our jobs back, they will be unemployed, and of course, they will be on the welfare rolls. They will be an economic drain on the country. What is the solution? Send them back now, where they belong, living in adobe huts—

Angrily, Lupe changes the radio station.

ANOTHER MAN'S VOICE

You will have a better life in Mexico. Take advantage of this opportunity. You will be able to help Mexico with the skills you have acquired in the United States. Also, by going to Mexico, a new middle class will emerge. In Mexico, you will find fertile land—

Lupe turns off the radio. She opens the window and yells outside.

LUPE

I am not going! I am staying here. This is my home. I am an American. Do you hear me, world? I am an A-m-e-r-i-c-a-n!

Juan enters. He closes the window.

JUAN
Lupe, come here.

He hugs her.

JUAN
Are you OK?

LUPE
The radio is saying insensitive and cruel things about Mexicans.

JUAN
I know. Lupe. That is one of the reasons we need to leave. What you just heard on the radio is nothing compared to what you will hear on the streets.

LUPE
I know, but it hurts.

JUAN
Employers are forbidden from keeping Mexicans on the job.

LUPE
I should be grateful. We have money and a car. I wish everybody were in our position.

JUAN
I agree. We are fortunate. Pablo and Sara have to take the train.

LUPE
Juan, I am sorry about the way I have been acting.

JUAN
We will be all right. Let's get ready to leave.

Blackout.

ACT II

<u>Scene 1</u>

Lights rise at the Mexican border. Juan, Lupe, Young Robert, Young Patty, and Grandma are seated as if in a car. Juan is driving.

> MEXICAN BORDER PATROL
> AGENT
> Do you have anything to declare?

> JUAN
> Yes. Please come to the car and check.

> MEXICAN BORDER PATROL
> AGENT
> Oh. You are one of those rich gringos.

> JUAN
> No, I just work hard.

Juan gets out of the car, walks to the rear, and opens the trunk.

> MEXICAN BORDER PATROL
> AGENT
> What is in that box?

> JUAN
> Just my tools.

MEXICAN BORDER PATROL
AGENT
You can't take them to Mexico.

JUAN
If I don't have these tools, I can't work.

MEXICAN BORDER PATROL
AGENT
Well, maybe that sewing machine will do.

JUAN
No! It belongs to my wife.

MEXICAN BORDER PATROL
AGENT
So…do you want to enter Mexico?

JUAN
No, I don't want to, but I am forced. I am an
American citizen. I was born in the United
States, but we are being sent back. You know
that very well.

MEXICAN BORDER PATROL
AGENT
Sir, I want the sewing machine.

JUAN
Take my tools.

Juan closes the trunk as the agent leaves. Juan reenters the car.

NOT FROM HERE, NOT FROM THERE

LUPE
Everything OK?

JUAN
Yes, we can cross the border now. Let's stop and rest before it gets dark. Grandma and the children need to walk.

Everyone exits the car. Three men approach.

MAN AT THE BORDER
Hey, gringo! Give us everything you have.

JUAN
I will give you what I have.

Juan pulls out a gun and starts shooting. Lupe, Grandma, and the children cower. The men run away.

LUPE
Grandma, children, get in the car!

Everyone gets back in the car.

LUPE
Juan, I am so scared. Let's wait for more cars, and we can drive in a caravan. We can protect one another.

JUAN
Good idea. We should drive only in the daytime.

LUPE
Did they charge at the border for our
things?

JUAN
Yes, but not so much.

LUPE
Are they charging the poor?

JUAN
No, the Mexican government tries to help
them by avoiding their tariffs. Lupe, look!
I just saw some wild animals. Let me hunt
them.

LUPE
No, no. Stay in the car. After what happened
with those men, I am scared.

JUAN
There are so many repatriates leaving the
United States that the restaurants along the
road are running out of food.

LUPE
Please, Juan, keep on driving until we see a
caravan. We can eat later.

JUAN
Look, Lupe! A caravan on the side of the
road. Let's join them.

LUPE
(smiling)
I feel so much better driving in a caravan.

JUAN
I agree.

LUPE
You know, we are returning one day.

JUAN
We will return. I promise you.

Blackout.

Scene 2

Lights rise. Juan, Lupe, Grandma, Young Robert, and Young Patty exit the car in a plaza in Guanajuato.

JUAN
You have to admit, this colonial city is
beautiful.

LUPE
Yes, look at that church. Juan, stop! Let me
read the name: "La Valenciana. Completed in
1788. Guanajuato was one of the richest cities
of the New World. The colonial residents were
very wealthy because of the silver mines."

Can we go in the church?

JUAN

You will have plenty of time to visit it. Let's get settled first.

LUPE

Look! Juarez Theater.

JUAN

Oh, it is beautiful. We will be happy here.

LUPE

I have never seen anything like it.

Blackout.

Scene 3

Lights rise. Juan and Lupe are sitting in a comfortable living room.

JUAN

Lupe, we have been here a month. Are you happy? Do you like this house?

LUPE

Yes, it is big and pretty, but it is temporary. My home is in the United States.

JUAN

Lupe, I will be right back. I am going to call the bank and ask them to send me our money. I saw a farm for sale. The farmland around here is some of the most productive in Mexico.

LUPE
Go on, but remember, this is temporary.

JUAN
Yes, I know.

Blackout.

Scene 4

Lights rise dimly on Juan and Lupe's living room. Juan enters, looking frustrated and defeated.

LUPE
Are you all right?

JUAN
Sit down. I have bad news.

LUPE
Haven't we had enough bad news? Tell me.

JUAN
The bank where we had our money has closed.

LUPE
You mean all we have left is this house?

JUAN
(sadly)
Yes, Lupe.

Blackout.

Scene 5

Lights rise on Juan and Lupe's living room. There is a knock at the door. Juan opens it. Pablo and Sara enter with Young Fernando. Juan hugs them warmly.

                    JUAN
          Pablo, Sara! We need some good news
          around here. Come on in. Look at
          Fernando. He has grown! The children are
          on the patio. Go and play with them.

Young Fernando exits.

                    PABLO
          Are you OK?

                    JUAN
          No. I called the bank in the United States,
          and it is closed. I lost all my money. I was
          going to buy a farm here. *(The women cry.)*
          The economic situation is bad in the United
          States.

                    PABLO
          It is bad all over the world. Rich countries.
          Poor countries. The unemployment rate in
          the United States is 25 percent.

                    JUAN
          Twenty-five percent?

                    PABLO
          Yes, it is that bad.

JUAN
How are you doing?

PABLO
Well....

JUAN
Come and live with us. We have extra rooms.
Robert and Patty will enjoy Fernando.

SARA
Thank you. We don't have anywhere else to
go.

They all hug each other.

JUAN
Please, sit down. Tell us about the train ride.

SARA
It was hard, but we made it fine. We met
some people who were worse off than us.
There are so many stories to tell you! Pablo,
tell them about the corral before we took
the train.

PABLO
Since thousands of people were being sent
to Mexico, there were not enough Mexican
trains to take them where they wanted to go.
So they put us in a corral.

LUPE
Just like animals!

SARA

Every day, we were ready to board the train.
As soon as we heard the train arriving, very
quickly all of us gathered our belongings
and held our children's hands. A few hours
later, we returned to the corral with great
sadness. We were told, "Maybe tomorrow.
The children thought this was all a game.

LUPE

So sad!

SARA

There was a young man. His name was Bruce
Gomez. He was like us, an American citizen.
He entertained the children. He taught
them the alphabet, to count, and to sing
children's songs. Since there were no pencils
or paper, he got sticks, and they wrote in the
clay. One day, there was only one seat left
on the train. The conductor told Bruce to
get in. When Bruce saw the sad faces of the
children, he jumped off the train and said
he would wait for another train.

JUAN

How long did you stay in the corral?

PABLO

Not long. Some said they were there for two
months.

Blackout.

Scene 6

Lights rise. Juan, Pablo, Lupe, and Sara are sitting in the living room and drinking coffee.

LUPE
Please, Sara, tell us another story tonight.
When I hear how those people suffered, I
feel so guilty to complain about my situation.

SARA
When we were at the border on the
American side, we saw many people thirsty
and hungry. Pablo told me to buy water and
food. I saw a couple in the processing center
sitting alone in the corner. They looked
scared.

Blackout.

Scene 7

Lights rise on the processing center. Sara walks toward Candelaria and Carlos, who are sitting on the floor.

SARA
Good afternoon. Would you like some
water?

CANDELARIA
Yes, yes. Thanks.

SARA
My name is Sara. May I sit near you?

CANDELARIA
Yes, please. I am Candelaria. This is my
husband, Carlos.

SARA
Where are you going?

CANDELARIA
To Santa Teresa. It is a town close to
Guanajuato.

SARA
We are going to Guanajuato, the capital!

CANDELARIA
Be sure to see the mummies. *(She smiles.)*

SARA
We have never been in Mexico.

CANDELARIA
You will be fine.

SARA
Where did you live in the United States?

CANDELARIA
In Illinois.

SARA
Were you ordered to repatriate?

CANDELARIA
No, no. *(lowering her voice)* We are illegals.

SARA
When did you come to the United States?

CANDELARIA
In 1914. My husband always wanted to go to the United States to work on cars. He wanted to go to Detroit. Mr. Ford was good to his workers, and Carlos loves machines.

SARA
Where did you settle in Illinois?

CANDELARIA
In East Saint Louis. We ran out of money, so we could not travel to Detroit. We settled in Illinois. The people were so nice, but after three years in East Saint Louis, there were riots.

SARA
I remember. I read something about them.

CANDELARIA
(sadly)
Below my window, someone killed a man.

SARA
How awful! I don't remember why they had riots.

CANDELARIA
There was an aluminum ore company. The white workers went on strike, so the company hired four hundred Negroes to

replace them. The whites resented the
Negroes taking their jobs.

SARA
(sadly)
We are like the Negroes now. They resent
us.

CANDELARIA
Yes, like East Saint Louis. We Mexicans took
their jobs, and the Americans did not have
any. In our case, it was not the strike but a
bad economy. I understand why they wanted
us out of there.

SARA
I wish I were as understanding as you. Tell
me, Candelaria. When you heard about
Mexicans being sent back to Mexico, what
did you do?

CANDELARIA
I took a bag, and very quickly, I put our
Sunday clothes in it. I knew in my heart
something was going to happen.

SARA
And your husband, what did he say?

CANDELARIA
(in a low voice)
He does not talk.

SARA
Is he OK?

CANDELARIA
Yes. His boss from the American Steel
Company sent the workers home on the
day of the riots. Carlos was running home,
and a girl with a club hit him on the head.
He does not know how long he was out, but
when some other men brought him home,
he had a bloody head.

SARA
I am so sorry.

CANDELARIA
He was unconscious for several days. When
he woke up, he could not talk.

SARA
What did you do?

CANDELARIA
I love him. Of course, I took care of him. He
can't talk, but he understands what I say.

SARA
Was he able to work?

CANDELARIA
Once he was better, I took him to see his
boss. I explained to him what happened.

He put him to work sweeping the floors. We were so grateful that he had a job. At the beginning, I took him to work very early in the morning, and then I would pick him up in the afternoon. However, a few months later, he walked to work all by himself. After a year, he was fixing machinery at the factory.

SARA
You are a brave couple.

CANDELARIA
As I said before, we are both illegals. When we found out we had to leave, I reminded Carlos that we were *Chichimecas*, the nomad people. We were sad, but we Indians accept our destiny.

SARA
I wish I could. Tell me more.

CANDELARIA
We were told to go to the train station in St. Louis. We walked there because we wanted to save money.

SARA
Was it very far?

CANDELARIA
No, but it took us almost a day. We walked slowly. It was very hot in July. We crossed the

Mississippi River on the Eads Bridge. Have you ever seen that bridge? It is big!

SARA
No, I haven't.

CANDELARIA
Let's laugh a little. I will tell you a story about the Eads Bridge.

SARA
Yes, tell me something pleasant.

CANDELARIA
The Eads Bridge was completed in 1874. They had an elephant from the circus test it by walking over the whole thing.

SARA
Are you kidding me?

CANDELARIA
No! People believe that elephants have an instinct that keeps them from stepping in places that are not safe.

SARA
Thanks for making me laugh.

CANDELARIA
It is the truth. The Eads Bridge is safe, and people have been using it for many years.

SARA
So you walked to St. Louis.

CANDELARIA
Yes. As I told you, it was hot and humid.
When we arrived at Union Station, we just
sat in a corner, looking at the mosaics, glass
windows, and archways. Sara, the station was
prettier than all the churches I have ever
seen!

SARA
And then you took the train to the border?

CANDELARIA
Yes. They gave us water and sandwiches.
They were so kind! Once we were on the
train, I heard people complaining. How
could we complain? Carlos and I were
illegals. We were able to work for many
years, eat well, and save money. And you,
Sara?

SARA
I am an American citizen. My parents,
grandparents, and great-grandparents were
all born in the United States. Our last name
is Martinez. Candelaria, it is an injustice to
send American citizens out of the country.
(*She cries.*)

CANDELARIA
I understand why Carlos and I had to leave.
We are illegals, but you are American

citizens. We had jobs, but I understand that American citizens need jobs. They have more right to work in their own country than we do.

The women sit in silence for a moment.

                    CANDELARIA
Do you have any children?

                    SARA
Yes, a boy named Fernando.

                    CANDELARIA
                    (sadly)
How lucky you are! I was pregnant once.

                    SARA
What did you have? A boy or a girl?

                    CANDELARIA
I don't know. The day we left Mexico, I was not feeling well. I did not say anything.

                    SARA
Why not?

                    CANDELARIA
Carlos had already made all the plans for the trip. Thank God, we were able to cross.

                    SARA
What did you do?

CANDELARIA

I kept on praying. I had to get well. I was
only two months' pregnant. I kept on
thinking, *When we arrive in Detroit, I will have a
nurse see me.*

SARA

Were you in pain?

CANDELARIA

When we arrived in East St. Louis, yes, I was
in pain. The day Carlos went looking for
a job, I had a miscarriage. I did not know
what to do. I just knelt and prayed. I also
poured a little water over its head to baptize
whatever it was, boy or girl. When Carlos
came home, I told him. We wrapped it in a
handkerchief very carefully and then dug a
little hole in the yard. We found two little
sticks and made a cross. We sat near the
little cross until it was very late and began
to snow. That night, I could not sleep, so
I stayed near a window where I could see
where the baby was buried. I talked to him
or her and said, "We love you."

Sara hugs her.

SARA

It was not meant to be.

CANDELARIA

I agree.

SARA
How did you feel afterward?

CANDELARIA
I felt terrible. The lady who rented the
room to us was a lovely German woman. She
came one day and saw me. She took me to
her German doctor, and he gave me free
medicine. I asked her how to say thanks.
She told me, "*Ich danke ihnen*." From that
day on, I called her the Danka Lady. Years
later, before we left the city, I knocked on
her door to say thank you for everything she
had done for us. She cried and told me, "*Geh
mit Gott*." Yes, Carlos and I went with God.
We are here, and I am grateful. Sara, don't
resent that you have to go to Mexico. There
is always a reason why things happen.

MAN'S VOICE
Time to board the train for people without
children.

Carlos and Candelaria get up to exit. Candelaria waves good-bye to Sara.

CANDELARIA
Bye, Sara, I hope to see you again.
Remember, forgive.

SARA
I don't know if I can. Bye.

Blackout.

Scene 8

Lights rise. Juan, Lupe, Pablo, and Sara are sitting in the living room.

SARA
Sometimes I think about Carlos and
Candelaria, and I wonder how they are
doing.

PABLO
I am sure they are doing fine. They are
survivors, and you know, Sara, we are, too.
Also, our son is healthy.

SARA
And young, very young. He is not aware of
the situation.

LUPE
Sara, tell us another story about before you
crossed the border. Your stories make me
feel better.

SARA
Well, I was saying how Fernando is so young
that he is not aware....

Blackout.

Scene 9

*Lights rise on people sitting aboard a crowded train traveling from
California to the Mexican border. Frank and Anthony are among them,
sitting next to each other.*

CONDUCTOR'S VOICE
Get on the train. Fast! Fast!

WOMAN'S VOICE
There are no seats left!

CONDUCTOR'S VOICE
Quiet!

The lights flicker. The train sounds as if it's on its way.

FRANK
Did you see the *King Kong* movie?

ANTHONY
Yes, I saw it. Mom took me for my
birthday.

FRANK
Did you get a present?

ANTHONY
Yes. A box of the new chocolate-chip
cookies. I ate some. I love them.

FRANK
What else did you get for your birthday?

ANTHONY
A game called Monopoly.

FRANK
I love that game. I wonder what kind of
music they have in Mexico.

ANTHONY
I like Bing Crosby.

FRANK
I like Carmen Miranda.

ANTHONY
Do you have a girlfriend?

FRANK
I liked one at my school. I may never see her
again. Anthony, I have an idea.

The boys lower their voices.

FRANK
I want to see the girl I told you about
again. I want to stay here in the United
States.

ANTHONY
I want to stay, too.

FRANK
I am going to the end of this car, and you
follow me. If someone asks where you
are going, tell them you are going to the
bathroom.

ANTHONY
And then what?

FRANK
When I jump, you follow me.

ANTHONY
I am scared.

FRANK
I will jump off when the train is slowing down.

ANTHONY
What if it does not slow down?

FRANK
Listen! I will jump anyway.

ANTHONY
OK.

FRANK
When you jump, roll over on one shoulder, and then roll into a ball. We will stay in our country. Repeat what I just said.

ANTHONY
Jump forward, roll on one shoulder, and roll into a ball. We will stay in the United States, and you will see the girl.

FRANK
Are you ready?

ANTHONY
Yes, but I am scared.

Frank stands and walks to the rear of the train car, then to the side of the stage. Anthony follows him. The train's noise indicates that it does not slow down.

MARIA TERESA H. DE HOLCOMB

FRANK
Jump!

ANTHONY
Here I go.

The boys jump offstage. Anthony's mother and Frank's mother enter the train car.

ANTHONY'S MOTHER
I wonder where my son, Anthony, is.

FRANK'S MOTHER
I think he went with my son to the bathroom.

ANTHONY'S MOTHER
Maybe they went to another car. You know how teenagers are, always looking for excitement.

FRANK'S MOTHER
We will see them before they cross the border.

WOMAN'S VOICE
Stop the train! I just saw two bodies on the ground.

CONDUCTOR'S VOICE
Quiet! Nobody would be stupid enough to jump from a moving train.

WOMAN'S VOICE
I told you, I saw two bodies. I beg you to stop the train!

CONDUCTOR'S VOICE
You are going to scare the passengers.

WOMAN'S VOICE
(*crying*)
But I saw two bodies. They looked like teenagers.

Complete silence.

Blackout.

Scene 10

Lights rise on a train station. People leave the train carrying their possessions as they wait to be processed before going to Mexico.

ANTHONY'S MOTHER
I don't see my son. Anthony, where are you?

FRANK'S MOTHER
Frank, answer me!

PABLO
Excuse me, ladies. Are you looking for your boys?

FRANK'S MOTHER
Yes, yes. They were on the train with us.

ANTHONY'S MOTHER
My son, Anthony, was wearing a blue shirt. He is tall with black hair.

FRANK'S MOTHER
My son, Frank, had a white shirt and also has black hair.

PABLO
Let me ask my wife if she saw them.

Pablo waves Sara over. She talks to the mothers. The mothers rush toward the side of the stage, as if to head back near the railroad tracks.

ANTHONY'S MOTHER
(yelling)
Anthony, where are you?

FRANK'S MOTHER
(yelling)
Frank, my boy, answer me!

The conductor steps in front of them.

CONDUCTOR
Come back! You are not allowed to leave the area. We have to process your papers.

ANTHONY'S MOTHER
No! We are going back. We are not leaving our boys. Maybe they are still alive.

CONDUCTOR
I am calling the police.

The women try to push past him.

FRANK'S MOTHER
Call the police! We don't care! We are going
to get our boys.

*Police officers enter and grab the women's arms to escort them back to the
processing center.*

FRANK'S MOTHER
My son did not want to leave the United
States. He was born here. He is only fifteen
years old.

ANTHONY'S MOTHER
Mine is sixteen years old.

*The officers seat the mothers on a bench in a corner of the stage. An officer
with a clipboard approaches them.*

OFFICER
Declare what you have.

ANTHONY'S MOTHER
I don't have anything.

OFFICER
How many people are traveling with you?

ANTHONY'S MOTHER
(sadly)
Only one.

FRANK'S MOTHER
I don't have anything. Only one person is
traveling.

OFFICER
Wait for the Mexican train. Don't run
away.

Sara walks toward the women.

SARA
Ladies, would you like some water, food?

ANTHONY'S MOTHER
Yes. Thank you. Could you sit with us for a
little while?

SARA
Sure.

Blackout.

Scene 11

*Lights rise on the processing center. Sara sits on a bench with Anthony's
mother and Frank's mother. A pregnant woman is in another part of the
center, at center stage.*

PREGNANT WOMAN
Does anybody have a knitting needle?

SARA
Excuse me a moment, ladies.

She walks toward the pregnant woman.

SARA
Yes, I have one. What do you need it for?

PREGNANT WOMAN
Come with me to the bathroom.

The women walk to the opposite end of the stage. Lights dim on Anthony's mother and Frank's mother.

PREGNANT WOMAN
Please, hand me the needle.

SARA
Here it is.

Sara reaches into her bag and withdraws the knitting needle. The woman takes it and bends over, as if to puncture herself between her legs. Sara quickly grabs her arm and takes the needle from her.

SARA
What are you doing?

PREGNANT WOMAN
(crying)
If I have the baby here in the States, it will be an American citizen, like me. When I return, I won't have to leave the baby in Mexico. Please, lady, help me?

Sara holds her.

SARA
You said you are an American, correct?

PREGNANT WOMAN
Yes, my family is from Alta, California. My great-grandparents used to say that in 1846,

it had a small population, and they lived in haciendas.

SARA

So your family lived in California before it became part of the United States?

PREGNANT WOMAN

Yes, and now they are sending me to Mexico because my last name is de la Madrid.

SARA

Come. Let's join the others. Don't put the baby's life in danger. Repeat to yourself, "I will return, and my baby will be an American citizen like me."

PREGNANT WOMAN

I hope so. Thank you.

SARA

It is our turn to board the train. Come with us.

PREGNANT WOMAN

No, thanks. I saw a woman on the way here with similar circumstances. I want to give her hope like you have given me. *(They hug.)* Good-bye.

Blackout.

ACT III

<u>Scene 1</u>

Lights rise in a corner of the dining room. Juan and Pablo are sitting at the table.

JUAN
Lupe tells me my children are unhappy here in Mexico. Robert and Patty are not accepted.

PABLO
My son told me he is not accepted, either.

Lights rise all over the stage. Lupe is cooking in a corner of the stage, in the kitchen. Young Robert enters.

YOUNG ROBERT
Mom, the school here is different.

LUPE
Different? How?

YOUNG ROBERT
When the teacher enters the classroom, we have to stand up. We can't sit down until she sits.

LUPE
I think it is good discipline and respect for the teacher.

YOUNG ROBERT
I prefer my school at home. I also miss my friends.

LUPE
Robert, what happened to your shirt?

YOUNG ROBERT
During recess, several boys called me *pocho*. I told them that I am an American and that I am here just for a little while. They told me the United States does not want Mexicans, and Mexico does not want us. Then they made a circle around me and sang, "Not from here, not from there." I don't want to go back. They also laugh when I speak Spanish and say, "*Pocho, pocho.*"

He cries.

LUPE
You are learning Spanish so fast. Remember the other day at the store, the lady could not understand me? You translated for me. I was so proud of you.

YOUNG ROBERT
OK, Mom. Now I understand. I will go and play with Fernando.

He runs off. Young Patty enters the kitchen.

YOUNG PATTY
Mom, I am sad today.

LUPE
Why?

YOUNG PATTY
The girls at school called me *gringa presumida.*

LUPE
What is *presumida?*

YOUNG PATTY
Something like a showoff. I want to have friends, but nobody wants to play with me. *(She cries.)* Also, they told me our home is big for only a few people. I think they are jealous.

LUPE
Yes, the house is big, and we are very fortunate.

YOUNG PATTY
When are we leaving? I miss my friends and my music. Mom, I miss everything! Let's go home.

LUPE
Are there any American girls your age at the school?

YOUNG PATTY
There were three. One of them moved to a ranch, and her parents put her to work in the fields.

LUPE
And the other two girls?

YOUNG PATTY
Since one of them did not speak Spanish, they put her in a lower grade. I don't see her anymore.

LUPE
And the other?

YOUNG PATTY
Her parents could not find work, so they could not pay the tuition. Mom, I want to go home. I don't like it here!

LUPE
(hugs her)
We will return. I promise.

Blackout.

Scene 2

Lights rise on Juan and Pablo as they talk in a corner of the living room.

> JUAN
> Pablo, the money is almost gone. You know,
> we have tried to find jobs, but we don't
> speak Spanish, and being foreigners is hard.
> I have an idea!

> PABLO
> Tell me. I am desperate.

> JUAN
> Come with me. We don't need to talk for
> this job.

They exit.

Blackout.

Scene 3

Lights rise on both men, who are holding brooms. They are smiling.

> JUAN
> Let's go and offer to sweep the front of
> those houses for those people.

> PABLO
> Great idea.

> JUAN
> We can talk to the mayor. Maybe we can
> sweep the whole city.

PABLO
Let's do it.

The lights dim, then rise again to show the passage of time. Juan and Pablo sweep.

JUAN
We have been working every day for fifteen hours, but it is not enough money to live on. The mayor refused to give us a job. I hate to tell you, but I have to sell the house.

PABLO
I understand. Everybody is suffering. In exchange for sweeping, people give us fruit and tortillas, but it is not enough.

JUAN
I know. I know. I have to tell Lupe.

Blackout.

Scene 4

Lights rise on Juan and Lupe's living room. Lupe is pacing.

LUPE
We are moving again? No! Grandma knows how to crochet. She will make things like baby booties. Patty will sell them at the market. Robert and Fernando will sell newspapers. Sara and I will sell food on the streets. I am not moving. Do you hear me, Juan?

Lights dim, then rise to show the passage of time.

> JUAN
>
> Lupe, we have to sell the house. We don't even have enough money to buy thread for Grandma to crochet. This is the worst situation we have ever experienced. I am sorry.

> LUPE
>
> Forgive me. I have not been happy since the day we found out we had to leave the United States. I have made your life miserable.

> JUAN
>
> I feel I am not much of a man. I cannot provide for my family. *(He cries.)* I feel like a failure. Yes, Lupe, I am a failure.

> LUPE
> *(caressing his face)*
> Juan, we are alive, we are healthy, and we love each other. Go and sell the house. It is fine.

Juan leaves and then returns.

> JUAN
>
> Lupe, I sold it. It was difficult. Nobody has any money. I lost money, and they also want the furniture. I told them OK. They want the house this Friday.

LUPE

It's fine. We will begin to pack. Tell Pablo
and his family. We all must stay together.

JUAN
(hugging Lupe)
Forgive me.

LUPE
I love you.

Blackout.

Scene 5

*Lights rise on a low-income housing project. Sara, Pablo, and Lupe carry
a few bundles of personal items. Young Patty, Young Robert, Young
Fernando, and Grandma carry a few belongings as well. Juan carries
Lupe's sewing machine.*

LUPE

All of you listen. The accommodations are
not fancy, but we have money for food. *(They
laugh.)* There is a shared bathroom in this
housing.

SARA

I just saw a creek where we can wash and
take baths. We don't have to use the shared
facilities, but I am worried about schooling.

LUPE

Grandma is always reading. She said she
always wanted to be a teacher. She can help

us. She was impressed about the story of the young man, Bruce, who taught the children to read at the corral.

SARA
Yes, yes. Lupe, we have hope.

Blackout.

Scene 6

Several years have gone by. Lights rise on a modest living room. Lupe is near her sewing machine, and Sara is knitting. Juan and Pablo enter.

JUAN
Pablo and I have good news for you.

LUPE
We need good news.

PABLO
The Japanese bombed Pearl Harbor!

LUPE
Sorry, boys, but that is not good news.

JUAN
The Americans are now involved in the war in Europe and Japan. They have declared war on Japan and Germany.

LUPE
Our country in war? Let's pray for our boys.

JUAN
I know wars are terrible, but now we can
return to our country and help.

SARA
How? I would do anything to help.

PABLO
Many of the small industries are being
converted into larger ones.

SARA
To make what?

JUAN
War materials: guns, tanks, ships, planes,
ammunition, and other supplies.

PABLO
The economy is booming. The defense
plants are employing men and women.

LUPE
Wait, Pablo! You said they are employing
women?

PABLO
Yes. Many of the men in the labor force are
being drafted, and others are volunteering
to serve in the military, so the industries
must employ women.

JUAN
(hugging Lupe)
They want us back. The defense plants pay
very well. Much better than before we left.

LUPE
I am good with my sewing machine. Juan.
Do you think I can operate a big machine?

JUAN
Of course you can. Lupe, we have hope.

LUPE
Finally! Sometimes I thought this day would
never come.

She dusts her sewing machine.

SARA
We need money to return.

JUAN
Pablo and I will work many more hours to
save extra money.

LUPE
Yes. Pablo and Juan, go to town and tell the
people that I know how to sew everything
from hems to wedding dresses.

SARA
You know how to sew wedding dresses?

LUPE
Sure. Just like a dress, but longer.

SARA
(smiling)
You are right. How can I help?

LUPE
You will sew the buttons.

The lights dim, then rise to show the passage of time. Lupe counts money. Patty, now a teenager, enters.

LUPE
I think we have enough. Let's go to where we belong.

PATTY
Mom, I need to talk to you. Remember Gabriel, the man I tutored in English?

LUPE
Sure. *(smiling)* His English is very good now.

PATTY
Mom, we have been boyfriend and girlfriend for a long time.

LUPE
Yes, I know.

PATTY
You know?

LUPE
Yes. What do you want to tell me?

PATTY
I hear we are returning to the United States.

LUPE
Yes, we are. Isn't it wonderful?

PATTY
Well, no. I am going to get married. I am
not going to the States.

LUPE
You are very young. Can you wait? I cannot
leave you here alone.

PATTY
Grandma wants to stay and live with Gabriel
and me.

LUPE
Grandma wants to stay? I don't believe it.

PATTY
Gabriel's father is coming tonight to ask Dad
for my hand.

LUPE
Tonight?

PATTY
Yes, and Grandma already made a few cookies.

LUPE
If that is what you want, then it is fine.
Let's talk to your dad.

Blackout.

Scene 7

Lights rise on a street in northern Mexico. Lupe, Juan, Sara, and Pablo are dressed for travel. Robert and Fernando, now teens, are with them.

JUAN
Well, we are in Chihuahua, and we are
running out of money. Let's take the bus
that stops in towns. We can work there, and
then with the money we earn, we can go
on to California. I am glad Fernando and
Robert are such good workers.

SARA
They are young and fast.

The men leave. The women sit on a bench.

LUPE
Remember when we left the United
States? It was 1930. The boys are now
teenagers.

SARA
They are so kind and handsome.

LUPE
Yes, they are. Sara, I think we are close to
the border. At night I can see the lights of
my country. Maybe it is my imagination.

SARA
Whatever it is, we are getting closer. The
only problem is, we don't have any money
left. I am getting hungry.

Lupe laughs.

SARA
It is not funny. I am hungry.

LUPE
Let's wait for the others. I have something to
tell you.

Juan, Pablo, and their sons return.

LUPE
Don't look so sad. I can tell by the
expressions on your faces that you did not
find any jobs and that you are hungry, too.

JUAN
Well, yes. We are hungry and very poor.

LUPE
Before we left Guanajuato, Patty's mother-
in-law came to see me. She gave me the *arras*

from her wedding. I did not want to
accept them. She told me she wanted to give
them to Patty, but she did not accept them,
either. She had everything she needed.
She told her to give them to someone who
really needs them, so she gave me thirteen
Centenarios.

SARA

Centenarios? I am going to pass out.

LUPE

We have enough money to go all the way to
Burbank and look for the defense plants.
Now we don't have to stop in every village to
look for work.

They all hug each other.

LUPE

Juan, please go to the bank and sell one
Centenario. We would love to go to a hotel
and take a bath. I know everybody agrees.

SARA

Where did you carry all that gold?

LUPE

Remember? I sewed a bag to put around
my neck. Well, it was for the money. It is so
heavy.

> JUAN
> Tomorrow we will cross the border. We don't have to worry. We have all the documents. We are legal! Well, we were never illegal.

Everybody laughs.

> JUAN
> Lupe, I will sell the coins and get dollars before we leave tomorrow.

> LUPE
> Yes, yes. They are heavy. My neck will not be sore anymore. *(She smiles.)*

Blackout.

Scene 8

Lights rise on a bus station at the Mexican border.

> MAN'S VOICE
> The Mexican government is charging a fee for you to leave Mexico.

Juan gives money to Lupe, Pablo, Sara, Robert, and Fernando.

> JUAN
> *(giving money to all)*
> All of you take this money and pay. We can't miss the bus. It's the last one of the day.

LUPE
Look, Juan, the ones who can't pay are in that
long line. They are going to miss the last bus.

JUAN
Quietly go and give them this money.

*The others buy bus tickets as Lupe walks up to a long line of people at the
side of the stage. She hands them money. Juan waits for Lupe. The bus's
engine starts.*

JUAN
Lupe, the bus is leaving!

LUPE
Coming!

*She leaves the line of people and buys a bus ticket. She hurries to Juan
and the others, who are seated in chairs as if they are aboard a bus.*

LUPE
I am here.

With tears in her eyes, she makes the sign of the cross.

LUPE
We are back. I missed my country.

Blackout.

ACT IV

<u>Scene 1</u>

Lights rise on Lupe, Juan, and Sara at a boarding house in the United States.

> LUPE
> Juan, can you take me tomorrow to see if my house is still there?

> JUAN
> Sure. Early in the morning, Pablo and I are going to Burbank to apply for jobs. We can go when we return.

> SARA
> Can I go, too? I wonder if my house is still there.

> JUAN
> Of course, Sara. Tell Pablo to come, too.

Blackout.

<u>Scene 2</u>

Lights rise on the old neighborhood. Lupe, Juan, Sara, and Pablo walk down the street.

> LUPE
> Sara, look! My house. They painted it. I like the colors. I wonder who lives here.

She rushes to the side of the stage and acts as if she's peeking in the window. Sara tugs her arm in excitement.

> SARA
> Let's go and look at my house. Oh, look!
> The sign says, "For Rent." Look, Pablo, we
> can rent our old house.

Lupe waves her over to the window.

> LUPE
> Sara, come and take a look. Your furniture is
> still there. The house looks abandoned.

> JUAN
> Let me call the real-estate agent.

Juan exits. The lights dim briefly, then come back up. Juan enters.

> JUAN
> The real-estate man is coming. He warned
> me that the house has been empty for years.
> Nobody has occupied it since the owners
> left.

> SARA
> Lupe and I know how to clean and repair
> things. We can also paint. This house can
> hold two families, and the children can
> attend their old school.

Blackout.

Scene 3

Lights rise. Juan waits outside a plant in Burbank. Pablo enters
excitedly.

> JUAN
>
> How was it?

> PABLO
>
> It went fine. I was tested, and I have a job!
> They pay well.

> JUAN
>
> I have a job, too. When they found out I
> speak some Spanish, they said I can test the
> skills of Mexicans before hiring them.

> PABLO
>
> After they see you, they will see me, and I
> will decide who will be hired.

Blackout.

Scene 4

Lights rise. Candelaria and Carlos sit at a table assembling parts. Juan
enters.

> JUAN
>
> Candelaria and Carlos, you did a very good
> job. Please wait here. Now you are going to be
> interviewed by the man who does the hiring.

Pablo enters.

CANDELARIA
Look, Carlos! It's our friend, Pablo.

She runs to Pablo and hugs him.

CANDELARIA
I will never forget you. You and your wife
were so kind to us when we were waiting to
cross the border to Mexico.

Juan looks at them.

JUAN
Where did you two meet?

PABLO
At the border, before we all took the train to
Mexico. Carlos, how are you doing?

Carlos smiles and nods.

CANDELARIA
He is doing great. Thanks.

JUAN
Let's talk business. Pablo, those two people
are very good. Both are very skilled. Carlos
was able to assemble parts for machines in
record time. Candelaria is very good, too.
Since she is detail-oriented, it took her a little
longer.

Juan hands Pablo some paperwork. Pablo reads the reports, then looks at Carlos and Candelaria.

PABLO
You two are hired. We need people like you. Please start tomorrow.

CANDELARIA
(in a low voice)
Juan, I must tell you…we are illegals.

JUAN
We need workers. We are at war. You two are very skilled. That is all we care about.

CANDELARIA
Thanks, Juan. Thanks, Pablo.

PABLO
When did you arrive?

CANDELARIA
This morning.

PABLO
Have you rented a place?

CANDELARIA
Well, not yet.

PABLO
We just rented the house we used to live in before we were repatriated. Why don't you come and stay with us?

CANDELARIA
Thank you. We accept, but we will rent an
apartment the day we get our paychecks.

PABLO
That is a deal.

They shake hands, smiling.

Blackout.

Scene 5

*Lights rise on Sara and Lupe in the living room of their rental house.
Pablo enters, ushering in Carlos and Candelaria.*

PABLO
Sara, I have a surprise for you.

SARA
A surpr—Candelaria!

She and Candelaria rush to hug each other. Sara hugs Carlos.

SARA
Lupe! This is the lady I told you about, the
one who told me I should forgive.

Lupe shakes hands with Candelaria and Carlos.

LUPE
Very nice meeting you.

CANDELARIA
How are the boys and Patty?

SARA
Fernando joined the army and became a member of the Third Infantry Division.

LUPE
Robert joined the marines. Patty got married and stayed in Mexico. Grandma stayed with Patty.

SARA
Let's all sit down. I am so happy to see you. I never saw you in Guanajuato. Did you go to Santa Teresa?

CANDELARIA
(sadly)
We went to my brother's house, but we had to leave.

Blackout.

<u>Scene 6</u>

Spotlight on Candelaria, alone on the stage.

WOMAN'S VOICE
Yes, Candelaria, you sent money every month, but now—

CANDELARIA
(looking around)
I am sorry. Our savings are gone. We gave
you all we had when we arrived.

WOMAN'S VOICE
Yes. Yes, I know. Your money is gone, and
you two are gone, too.

CANDELARIA
We have sent you money since 1914, and
now we need help.

WOMAN'S VOICE
I don't run charities. Get out! I don't want
to see you anymore. Out, out!

Lights rise on the living room of the rental house, showing Carlos, Sara, Pablo, Juan, and Lupe with Candelaria.

SARA
Did you have a plan?

CANDELARIA
No. I tried to understand her. We were in
her way. One day when I returned from
looking for a job, I saw a bundle of my
things outside the door. I went in and took
Carlos by the hand, and we started to walk.

SARA
Did you walk again like you did from Illinois
to Missouri?

CANDELARIA

No, we took a bus. We were hungry when we arrived. I saw two nuns going into a stone building. I ran to them and asked for help. They were not surprised to see us. There were many people in the same situation. I asked for job in exchange for a little food. They invited us in. I kissed their hands. I was so grateful. They brought us food, but I told Carlos we had to earn the food. There were two brooms near the door. We swept the whole patio and entrance. When the nun returned to get the dishes, she saw that we had not eaten anything. She asked why. I told her we had to do something to pay for the food before eating it. I think she was impressed with how the patio and entrance looked, so she brought an older nun to see it. To make a long story short, we lived in the convent for many years. As soon as the first bell rang every morning, we started to sweep. *(smiling)* We swept so much, the nuns had to buy brooms quite often!

One day, I heard there was a labor shortage in the United States because of the country's entry into World War II. The defense plants needed workers. Imagine, they were even hiring women! I told the nuns about my plans. They gave us *escapularios* to protect us. I felt as sad when I left the nuns as when I left the Danka Lady in Illinois. We boarded the bus headed for Tijuana.

SARA
Were you nervous?

CANDELARIA
I was so nervous that I even lost my feeling
of excitement. We did not have documents.
I kept on thinking, *What if we have to go back
to Guanajuato? What if the nuns already hired
somebody to sweep the convent?* I was shaking,
and we were all so hungry. We went to a
restaurant that had mariachis. Some marines
were having so much fun. One of the girls,
a friend of the marines, said to me, "Hello,
little lady." She was so tall!

She stands on tiptoe and raises her arms to demonstrate.

CANDELARIA
We talked to them. They were funny.
They had been drinking. They asked about
our lives in Mexico. I told them we were
going to Burbank to work and support the
American war effort. I had to tell them we
were illegals. They laughed and told us,
"Come with us. We are going to San Diego,
and the Border Patrol is not strict. You
people deserve a break, and we are going to
help you."

We all got in their car, and the Border
Patrol smiled and made the sign to cross. I
started to cry. Such kindness from strangers!
Before we said thanks, I took out my

escapulario, which was the only thing I had, and gave it to the tall lady. She put it on like a bracelet. We waved good-bye. We took the bus from San Diego to Los Angeles, and then to Burbank to apply for work at the defense plant. That is my story. We are here, and now we have jobs.

Blackout.

Scene 7

It is years later. Lights rise inside the rental house. Sara and Pablo sit with Fernando. Juan and Lupe enter. Fernando struggles to stand and greet them.

FERNANDO
Lupe, Juan, good to see you. I am sorry about Roberto. I still miss him. He was like a brother to me.

Lupe bursts into tears and hugs Fernando.

FERNANDO
I am sorry I brought it up.

LUPE
No, no. I am sorry that you lost your leg in combat.

FERNANDO
I am fine now. When I finish college, I will help the veterans. Lupe, if my mother does

not mind, I will take you as a second mother.
Can I be your son?

LUPE
Of course. You will be the grandson I never
had. A little older, but my grandson.

FERNANDO
Well....

SARA
What is it, Fernando?

FERNANDO
Well, just before Roberto left to go overseas
in 1943—

PABLO
Speak up, Fernando!

LUPE
I beg you. Just before he left, what?

FERNANDO
Roberto said, "If something happens to
me, I want you to know my girlfriend is
pregnant."

LUPE
I did not know he had a girlfriend. Did he
get married?

FERNANDO
No. I know her. She loved Roberto. She
is nice.

LUPE
Who is she? Is she someone we know?

FERNANDO
Well, no. The baby—

LUPE
Is it a boy or a girl?

JUAN
Where does she live? Give us the address!

FERNANDO
Yes, I know where she lives.

JUAN
We are all going there right now.

FERNANDO
Maybe I should go first. Her family is a
little…let's say difficult.

LUPE
No, we are all going right now.

SARA
Let me help you with your crutches.

The lights dim, then rise to show both families standing outside a house. Juan knocks on the door. Mrs. Smith opens it.

MRS. SMITH
Sorry, we don't have any jobs for you. Leave the neighborhood.

She closes the door. Juan knocks again. She flings the door open.

JUAN
Madam, sorry to disturb you, but I have something very important to ask you.

MRS. SMITH
We don't associate with you people. I am going to call the police.

JUAN
I beg you, señora. Please, listen to me. Your daughter had a child with my son.

MRS. SMITH
I don't know what you are talking about.

JUAN
She had a child with my son. He was killed in action in the South Pacific.

Mrs. Smith starts to close the door, but Megan screams. Megan tugs the door open and pushes her mother behind her.

MEGAN
Is Robert dead? When did he die?

LUPE
Six months ago.

MRS. SMITH
She does not have a baby from a Mexican.
There is no child in this house.

MEGAN
There is no child here.

LUPE
Did you have a child?

MEGAN
Yes, a beautiful boy. I am sorry about my
mother's behavior. She always disapproved
of your son, but Roberto was good to me.

LUPE
Excuse me, where is the baby?

MEGAN
(crying)
I am sorry to tell you…my mother ordered
me to put him in an orphanage.

LUPE
In an orphanage?

Mrs. Smith
(yelling behind Megan)
I warned her about him. We don't mix with
Mexicans.

MEGAN
Mother! These people are polite. Show a
little class!

MRS. SMITH
Inferior people.

The families stiffen, but they say nothing.

MEGAN
Since Robert was a Catholic, I put him in a
Catholic orphanage.

LUPE
Please, let's go and see my grandson. Is he
still there?

MEGAN
I don't know.

Blackout.

Scene 8

*Lights rise in an office at the orphanage. Megan sits with Juan, Lupe,
Pablo, Sara, and Fernando.*

MEGAN
I come by here every day, but I have not
seen him since I gave him up. I know that
what my mother and I did seems cruel. I
will never get over it. That is why I never
go inside and inquire. It would be too
painful.

LUPE
What if he was adopted? Sara, let's pray.

Lupe and Sara clasp hands.

LUPE
Dear God, let me hold this child of my dead son in my arms. My son gave his life for our country. I beg You, dear God, to let me have a part of him. Amen.

A nun enters, smiling.

NUN
Welcome, everybody! Please sit down. What can I do for you?

MEGAN
(crying)
I brought you my baby....

NUN
Tell me more about him. We get so many children because of the economic situation over the last decade.

MEGAN
(crying)
He was a beautiful boy. He had straight, coal-black hair. Beautiful dark eyes.

LUPE
(mumbles)
Just like his father.

MEGAN
Tell me, Sister, has anybody adopted him?

NUN
I think I know which child you are referring to. Nobody adopts Mexican babies. Please, one moment.

The nun leaves and returns with a toddler boy. Everybody looks at him as he holds on to the nun's habit.

MEGAN
Sister, I am the mother.

NUN
Yes, I remember you now. The day you brought him in, he was just a few hours old. I told you to please give him to me, and you just kept on telling me, "Let me hold him a little longer." When you finally gave him to me, it was late, and the orphanage was ready to close. You kissed him and told me, "Would you please call him Robert?" We did. We call him Robertito. Little Roberto.

MEGAN
I will never forget that day. Sister, these people are the grandparents. They want to adopt him.

The lights dim, then rise to show the passage of time. Megan arrives at the rental house and kisses Lupe and Juan on the cheek.

MEGAN

I would like to know if I can see Robertito.

LUPE

Of course. Robertito, your mom is here.

MEGAN

You adopted him. You are the mother.

LUPE

No, you are the mother. I am the grandma.

MEGAN

Thank you. At first, I thought I would not be able to handle this situation.

LUPE

We all understand. Do you want to hold him?

MEGAN

I don't know. I held him for only a few hours after he was born.

LUPE

When you are ready, you will.

Blackout.

Scene 9

Lights rise on the living room of the rental house. Megan is playing with the toddler boy.

MEGAN

Señora Lupe, do you think I can take
Robertito to my mother's house?

LUPE

Of course! You don't need my permission.
He is your son.

*The lights dim, then rise to show Megan outside her home, with the
toddler in her arms.*

MEGAN

Mom, look how cute he is.

MRS. SMITH

Cute? You call that cute? His skin is dark,
and his hair looks like that of a porcupine.

MEGAN

Look, Mom, he is smiling at you. If he could
understand what you are saying, he would
be sad and cry. Mom, how could you be so
cruel?

Megan turns to leave.

MEGAN

I am leaving this house, and I don't ever
want to see you again. You are a cruel and
racist lady!

*The lights dim, then rise to show Megan and the toddler back at Lupe
and Juan's house.*

MEGAN
Can I stay here? I cannot go to my mother's
house. I prefer not to tell you the reasons.

LUPE
Yes, please. Stay with us. We would be so
happy. Family is what it is all about.

MEGAN
I will work.

JUAN
Enjoy, do not worry about anything.

The lights dim, then rise to show the passage of time.

MEGAN
I have been thinking about my mother.

LUPE
I have, too.

MEGAN
I would like to go and see her.

LUPE
That is wonderful. It is not good to break
ties with the family.

MEGAN
I know. I like that about Mexicans.

Blackout.

Scene 10

Lights rise. Megan arrives alone at her mother's house.

MRS. SMITH
Megan, it is good to see you. How are you?

MEGAN
Fine, Mom.

Silence.

MEGAN
Are you going to ask me how your grandson is doing?

MRS. SMITH
Grandson? That dark-skinned baby you had with that man of Mexican race?

MEGAN
Mexican is a nationality, not a race. Yes, Mom, I have a son whose father was a mestizo.

MRS. SMITH
Mes…what?

MEGAN
M-e-s-t-i-z-o is a person of mixed Indian—

MRS. SMITH
With black?

MEGAN
No, Mom. The father was a mix of Indian
and European—

MRS. SMITH
Shame on you!

MEGAN
Mom, your family was European, correct?

MRS. SMITH
Yes, they emigrated from Europe to the
United States. They needed jobs.

MEGAN
The Mexicans are the hungriest and poorest
immigrants now, Mom! The ones who were
doing well, before the repatriation, were
sent back and lost everything they had.
Some of them were American citizens with
Spanish last names.

MRS. SMITH
We needed their jobs. You are forgetting
something: we are white. We are white! Look
at you! Your skin is pale and white, not like
your hairy porcupine. Mexicans are dark.
We do not look like dark people. Do you
hear me? I am not a grandmother of a dark
child.

Megan turns to leave.

                    MEGAN
          Mom, your attitude is disgusting, and I don't
          think you will ever change. I feel so sorry for
          you.

Blackout.

Scene 11

Lights rise at Juan and Lupe's house. Megan sits quietly.

                    LUPE
          Megan, you seem sad.

                    MEGAN
          No, I am fine.

                    LUPE
          Juan and I were thinking. We are getting
          old. Thank God Juan has a very good job.
          Patty does not need any money. Gabriel is
          very rich. You are a very smart girl. What do
          you want to do with your life?

                    MEGAN
          I love history. Every time I hear you talk, I
          want to learn more and more. I would like
          to go to college and then teach the truth,
          good and bad, of history.

                    JUAN
          Megan, you are our daughter. We want to
          help you. You have brought us so much

happiness. If you want, you can go to
college. We will pay for it and help you with
Robertito. We would love to take care of
him.

>MEGAN
>*(hugging both grandparents)*
>Thank you! Robert would be happy.

Blackout.

Scene 12

*It is years later. Lights rise on a classroom. Megan is teaching. She holds
a gold star-shaped medal with a blue ribbon.*

>MEGAN
>Many of you don't know about a chapter in
>American history. Maybe your grandparents
>have told you about repatriation. Look at
>this medal.
>
>A brave American man with Mexican roots
>was killed in battle. He saved the lives of
>several soldiers. A few months later, he
>was awarded the Congressional Medal of
>Honor posthumously. His family was born
>in this country and goes back for several
>generations. They were all American
>citizens. But during the Depression of
>the 1930s, even legal American citizens
>of Mexican descent were sent back to
>Mexico.

The situation in Mexico was terrible. Most of the American citizens did not speak Spanish and had never even been to Mexico. They were accepted neither by the Mexicans there nor the Americans here. In other words, they were not from here, and they were not from there. They found themselves as people without a country. When they were allowed to return to the United States, their own country, their children joined the armed forces to defend the country they loved.

This man, in spite of all of this, died for the country that never accepted him as a first-class citizen. So students, this second-class citizen received a first-class honor from the military for his heroic service as a United States Marine.

She holds up the medal. Complete silence.

Blackout.

Scene 13

Lights rise, later at home. Robertito kisses Megan as she enters.

ROBERTITO
Mom, what did you teach today?

MEGAN
I told a story about your father.

Lights dim to blackout.